Contents

C000198071

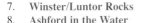

It is strongly recommended that walkers wear suitable clothing and footwear, appropriate to the walk and conditions that can sometimes be encountered on open moorland and exposed hillsides. This usually means walking boots, outer waterproof/windproof jacket and a type of walking trousers (not jeans) along with a warm sweater and other body clothing. A small day rucksack with some food/drink and your personal items are also strongly recommended.

The description of a route or track is not evidence of a right of way. Compass bearings shown in this book are given as magnetic bearings. All distances are shown in metres.

It is recommended that a compass and the following map are used in conjunction with this book. Ordnance Survey Explorer No. OL24 The Peak District - White Peak Area

To help shorten the text the following abbreviations have been used throughout: -

PF = Public Footpath	LT = Left	S = Start
PB = Public Bridleway	RT = Right	P = Park
CP = Car Park	RD = Road	FB = Footbridge
GR = Grid Reference	Mts = Metres	

The walks have been graded for difficulty with **1** being the easiest/flattest to **5** the most demanding in terms of ascents/descents: -

Walk No.1 = **3 - 4**	No.4 = **3**	No 7 = **1**
No.2 = **3**	No.5 = **3**	No.8 = **2**
No.3 = **2**	No.6 = **3**	No.9 = **4**

I hope you enjoy this selection of walks, which are spread throughout the Matlock and Bakewell areas. All are undulating but the majority are not too demanding, with excellent scenery and views from the hills. I hope you get as much pleasure from walking them as I did.

Brian Smailes

ISBN 1-903568-55-2

Walk 1 Nine Ladies Stone Circle Walk
Walk Time 2hrs 10min   **Distance** 3.2miles/5.1km
Start In School Lane, Rowsley. GR. 257658

1. Walk along the lane following the sign for the craft centre. Cross the bridge over the river, follow the signpost **PF** to Stanton Lees. Keep on the main narrow lane as it winds round and through Holly Wood.

2. When you arrive at the gates of Stanton Woodhouse, a large house, follow the winding track **RT** then **LT** to pass Stanton Woodhouse Farm. Go through the 5-bar gate and follow the slightly worn track round the field as you ascend towards Endcliffe quarry. You pass between two stone posts and you may see the tower on top of the hill.

3. Continue ascending the grass path and go straight through the metal gate, do not go off on the path bearing to the **RT**. Once through the gate you walk between two wire fences, walking to the **RT** of the old quarry. Continue round the quarry to the **RD** at the far side then turn **LT** into the village of Stanton Lees.

4. In the village, take the **RT** fork signposted Birchover and follow this undulating, mostly ascending **RD** to join another **RD** beside a chapel. Turn **RT** here still ascending the hill. Pass the sign on the **RT** for Stanton Moor Edge; continue round the bend a little further to a step stile on your **RT** with a stone post on each side of it.

5. Cross the stile, take a general bearing of 24°M then ascend the hillside between the bracken and onto moorland on high ground. Follow your bearing and stay on the main stony path as you walk towards Stanton Moor Plantation. Just as you start to walk in the woodland, look to your **LT** to see the Nine Ladies Stone Circle, continue on the main path again by the edge of the woodland towards Lees **RD**.

6. Go through three small wooden gates as you near Lees **RD**. Turn **LT** to descend the **RD** to the far side of Sheepwalk Wood. Just before arriving at the first houses of the village, turn **RT** on a **PF** towards Stanton cricket club. Walk between Sheepwalk Wood and the cricket ground. Continue into the wood keeping to the **LT** side as you follow the worn path down to the far end to emerge on Pilhough Lane.

7. On the lane, turn **RT** passing Beighton Houses then just past a viewing point on the **LT**, turn **LT** to descend a field on bearing 24°M. Continue crossing several fields to emerge on a steep narrow lane. Turn **LT** onto the lane which has two sharp bends in it.

8. A **PF** sign on the **RT** on the second bend beside Dove House Farm points along a grass track and through a narrow opening. Go through then follow the narrow worn grass path around the hillside. Go through a small gate towards a copse then ascend through another gate into the copse. Ascend through a third gate out of the copse into a field.

9. Take a bearing of 62˚M then walk round the mound known as Peak Tor. Going initially up, then further round descending to the far **LT** corner by the river. Exit through a farm gate onto the minor **RD**. Turn **LT** on the **RD** and walk along by the river to the bridge near where you started, turn **LT** over the bridge back into School Lane.

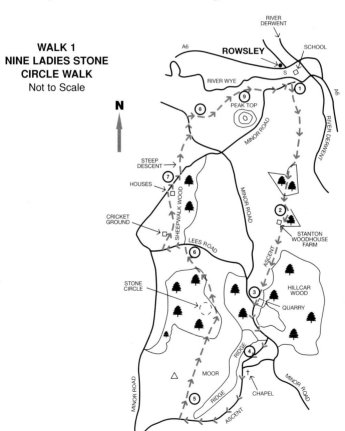

WALK 1
NINE LADIES STONE
CIRCLE WALK
Not to Scale

Walk 2 Snitterton Round

Walk Time 1hr 30min   **Distance 3.6miles/5.75km**

Start Large car park beside Matlock Railway Station.
GR. 297602

1. Look for **PF** sign in **CP** to Oker, which takes you on a tarmac path by the river, passing trees for 1.2Km. Continue in a straight line past new building works and an asphalt factory. You come to a stile after the last factory, which you cross then continue ahead. Keep on path close by the river, don't take the path off to **LT**. Continue on path over next field to **RT** side of houses ahead.

2. Emerging on a **RD** by the houses, turn **RT** taking you towards the river again. Follow the lane round anti-clockwise to where the narrow **RD** finishes. A small derelict barn is on the **LT**. Take the path just before it on **LT** ascending steeply through trees up towards Oker, emerging beside some houses on an access **RD**.

3. Continue across to a stile on higher ground, cross then follow the slightly worn path between the trees over the brow of the hill. Cross another stile before meeting another track, this crosses **LT** to **RT** by a waymark post. Turn **LT** then after a short distance turn **LT** again over a stile leading down steps into a short piece of woodland.

4. Continue down through the bushes, descending to the **RD** you can see below at the far corner of the field. Cross a stile onto the **RD** and walk for 30Mts to the junction. Turn **LT** then **RT** onto a **PF**. Continue ahead to Snitterton and walk along a narrow path between houses. As you emerge on a **RD**, turn **RT** along a lane, look for a **PF** sign to Leawood Farm and walk up the access **RD**.

5. Cross a cattle grid on the **RD**, stay on the track to where it divides. Take the **LT** fork to ascend steeply to Jughole Wood, go over a ladder stile. You come to another stile, turn **LT** then cross over a further stile walking straight across the field. You are now heading over a series of fields towards Masson.

6. As you approach Masson, you see the large house in front of you. Keep to the **RT** of it alongside the fence. Look for a concealed opening taking you over a stone stile into a field. You see another house where you bear **LT** onto the access **RD**. Turn **RT** on the access **RD** still descending past a farm and houses to the main **RD** beyond.

7. At the **RD**, turn **RT**, a sign states Welcome to Matlock. Continue along the **RD** back into Matlock.

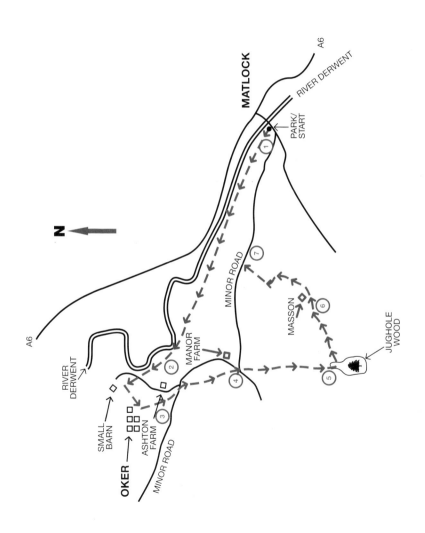

WALK 2
SNITTERTON ROUND
Not to Scale

N

MATLOCK

A6

RIVER DERWENT

PARK/START

1

MINOR ROAD

7

MASSON

6

JUGHOLE WOOD

5

A6

RIVER DERWENT

MANOR FARM

2

4

SMALL BARN

ASHTON FARM

3

OKER

MINOR ROAD

Walk 3 Haddon Fields Walk

Walk Time 2hrs 30min   **Distance** 4.2miles/6.75km

Start On Agricultural Way on outskirts of Bakewell just off A6.
GR. 223678

1. Start by the bridge over the river where a sign states 'no pedestrian access'. A footpath leads off to the LT behind a row of houses and past allotments. Continue along the narrow path behind the houses, cross a cul-de-sac and continue into a recreation park. Bear RT towards the riverside and as you walk along the bank, you see a bridge over the river on your RT.

2. Cross the bridge then walk across the CP to cross another small bridge in front of the coach park and cattle market. Emerging on the RD, turn RT and cross a cattle grid, a sign points to Haddon Hall. Continue along the RD then as it bends RT, keep straight on by the LT hand hedge following the PF sign over stiles and generally by the river.

3. Cross a small FB still on the obvious path then cross a stile before ascending a short flight of steps. Go through a wooden gate to emerge on a lane. Turn RT then LT after 20Mts to continue on the PF by the river. Stay on this narrow path until you emerge on the A6 RD.

4. Turn LT at the RD continuing to Haddon Hall entrance. Opposite there is a PF sign pointing RT just past the building there. Continue on this PF, through a 5-bar gate to ascend the hillside going through a small gate on route. Keep in the same direction until you come to an old barn. Cross the stone steps next to the 5-bar gate then turn RT.

5. Keep the stone wall just to your RT and continue in this direction to emerge on a RD. Continue again in the same direction on the RD, passing Noton Barn Farm. Just past the farm where the RD bends, look for a PF bearing RT across the fields. Where you see the sign with two arrows on it, take the LT fork in the direction of the houses.

6. Nearing the houses, cross a stile on the RT, descend the field, and go through a gate towards a house with a tower. Descend to the brook at the bottom; cross it then walk clockwise by the wall to pass a school on your LT. Halfway past the school go through a kissing gate on your RT.

7. This takes you down past the RT side of the churchyard, and through Catcliff Wood. You descend steeply to the RD at the bottom. Go through a kissing gate then turn LT on Park View and at the junction there turn RT, descending to the main RD.

8. Turn RT walking the short distance back to the start.

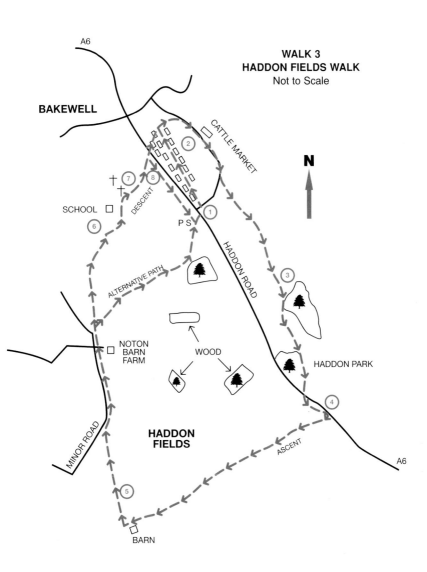

A6

BAKEWELL

WALK 3
HADDON FIELDS WALK
Not to Scale

N

CATTLE MARKET

② ①

⑦ ⑧

SCHOOL

DESCENT

⑥

P S

HADDON ROAD

③

ALTERNATIVE PATH

WOOD

HADDON PARK

NOTON
BARN
FARM

④

MINOR ROAD

HADDON
FIELDS

ASCENT

A6

⑤

BARN

Walk 4: Rowsley/Edensor Circular

Walk Time: 2hrs 45min. **Distance: 5miles/8km**

Start: Beside the Post Office in Rowsley Village. GR. 255659

1. From the Post Office, head to the top of the lane, passing the last house. The lane turns into a track as it bends round anti-clockwise, ascending towards Bouns Corner (wood). On reaching the wood you arrive at a metal barrier, go round it and carry on the main wide woodland track that bears off **LT**. Continue on through a clearing to the far side then descend keeping a stone wall on your **LT** side.

2. You come to another metal barrier, go around it then turn **RT** by a small metal barrier, following a wooden bridleway sign to Chatsworth. You are now ascending a narrow path through woodland again then onto a wider track still ascending in the same direction.

3. At a green sign for Haddon Estate, bear **RT** to ascend to the top of the wood. As you reach the top your path gets narrower and there is a stone wall on your **RT** side. There are good views to your **LT** over the trees towards Bakewell in the valley. Continue until you see an opening on your **RT** with a stone post on each side. Turn into here and follow the winding path through the wood to the far side.

4. You emerge by a broken stone wall, and cross a ladder stile into a field with good views over the fields below. From the ladder stile take a bearing of 24°M and descend the field on the worn path to Calton Plantations. At the wood, go through a 5-bar gate then walk immediately **RT**, descending alongside the wood and a stone wall to pass behind Calton House.

5. The path bends **LT** and ascends towards a barn and another wood. Go through a 5-bar gate which takes you on a track through New Piece Wood. At the far side of the wood, cross stone steps into the field then set a bearing of 24°M again to descend into the village of Edensor.

6. You see the river off to your **RT** as you descend to the **RT** of the houses and on to the main **RD** at the far side. At the **RD** turn **RT** walking to the bend, then **LT** following the **RD** towards the bridge over the River Derwent in front of Chatsworth House.

7. At the bridge, turn **RT**, taking a feint path, which cuts across the field by the river going south back towards Rowsley. At the next bend in the river, stay on the feint path keeping close by the river all the way to the bridge over the river at Calton Lees.

8. Go through an opening near the bridge onto the **RD** then turn **RT** going round the house opposite, then follow a sign 'footpath to Rowsley'. Ascend the short path through the copse up to a **CP** by a **RD** then turn **LT** on a metalled **RD**. Continue into Calton Lees village.

9. Turn **LT** in the village signposted Rowsley, walking between the farm and houses then turn **LT** over stone steps again to Rowsley on the Heritage Way. Now on a narrow path by a stone wall leading towards the river again, you go over a step stile. Turn **RT** going over several fields to a stile close by the river.

10. You now walk through a short piece of woodland and as you emerge at the far side you see some houses on the outskirts of Rowsley. Continue on the path then access track which eventually emerges by a farm on the **RD** just above the Post Office in Rowsley.

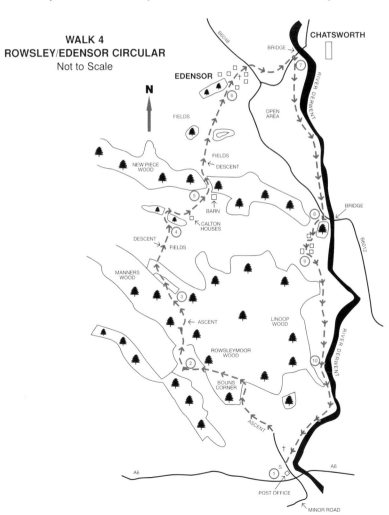

WALK 4
ROWSLEY/EDENSOR CIRCULAR
Not to Scale

CHATSWORTH

B6048

BRIDGE

RIVER DERWENT

EDENSOR

N

7

OPEN AREA

FIELDS

6

NEW PIECE WOOD

FIELDS
← DESCENT

BRIDGE

5

BARN

B6012

CALTON HOUSES

4

8

DESCENT
→ FIELDS

9

MANNERS WOOD

LINOOP WOOD

3

← ASCENT

RIVER DERWENT

ROWSLEYMOOR WOOD

2

BOUNS CORNER

10

ASCENT

A6

A6

†

1

S

POST OFFICE

MINOR ROAD

Walk 5 Golf Course & Manners Wood Circular

Walk Time 2hrs 10min   **Distance 5.2miles/8.3km**

Start On Agricultural Way just off A6 on outskirts of Bakewell. GR. 223678

1. Start by the bridge over the river where a sign states 'no pedestrian access'. A footpath leads off to the **LT** behind a row of houses and past allotments. Continue along the narrow path behind the houses, cross a cul-de-sac and continue into a recreation park. Bear **RT** towards the riverside and as you walk along the bank, you see a bridge over the river on your **RT**.

2. Cross the bridge then walk across the **CP** to cross another small bridge in front of the coach park and cattle market. Emerging on the **RD**, turn **RT** and cross a cattle grid, a sign points to Haddon Hall. Continue along the **RD** until it bends **RT**; keep straight along by the **LT** hand hedge following the **PF** sign over stiles. You come to a narrow **FB** on your **LT** and a **PF** sign where you turn **LT** to ascend a field to a **PB** running alongside a wood.

3. On the **PB**, which is a stony access track, turn **LT**, walking towards Bakewell, with a wood on **RT** then on both sides. You emerge on Coombs **RD** beside an old railway bridge. Bear **LT** then immediately **RT** up onto an old railway line. On the path at top, turn **LT** and walk until you come to a stone bridge over the path. Just past there is a **PF** on your **RT**.

4. Ascend the steps to top and turn **LT** ascending by the golf course. Continue ascending between the fences on either side towards the wood. On reaching the wider open area of the golf course, bear slightly **LT** ascending on a stony winding path into the wood. It is important to keep directly ascending, do not take any other horizontal paths you may see.

5. At the top of wood go through a small wooden gate to emerge into a large field. Follow the worn path, ascending the field over the brow of the hill. There are good views looking back to Bakewell. You see a copse of trees in centre of field, walk to **RT** of it then go through the 5-bar gate ahead, (not the smaller gate on **LT**).

6. You are now on a worn grass path along a long field on high ground. You eventually cross a stile then bear **RT** across the field to the corner of the woodland ahead and a mound near it. Walk around the **LT** side of the wood then you see a ladder stile beside a 5-bar gate.

7. Cross into the wood following the distinct winding path through the wood then into the next section of woodland and through to emerge on a ridge beside two large stone posts, with good views ahead. Turn **LT** here, walking on the distinct path, keeping the stone wall on your **LT**. You soon start to descend steeply through the wood.

8. Stay on this descending path; do not turn onto any other path. Where the path forks continue on the descending path. You are now on a track leaving the wood. At a junction of three paths/tracks, bear **RT**, leaving a small wood to your **LT**. The access track winds **RT** following a sign for Bakewell.

9. Continue up then down past Bowling Green Farm when you leave the track to walk on a narrow path. Go through a small gate then follow the path by a metal fence going through another gate to descend onto a metalled access **RD**. Turn **LT** to descend the **RD**, staying on it until you reach the river at the bottom.

10. As you reach the bend in the **RD** just before the river, you see a **PB** sign on **RT**. Go through the small gate there following the lower path nearby the river, looking for the small waymarker posts. The path leads **LT**, close by the river. Descend three steps over a small grass section then cross a stile close by the river.

11. Continue on the path by the river to rejoin the path you came on. Walk along near the river and over the stiles until you reach the **RD** (Agricultural Way). At the **RD**, turn **LT**, crossing the bridge over the River Wye. You have now reached the point you started at.

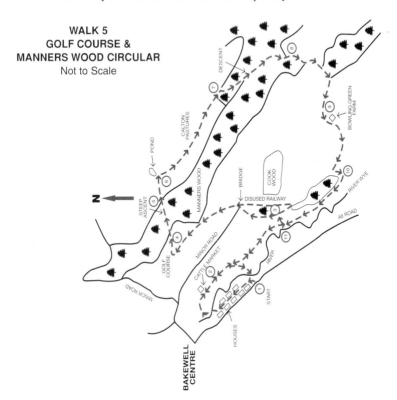

WALK 5
GOLF COURSE &
MANNERS WOOD CIRCULAR
Not to Scale

Walk 6 Tansley/Riber Circular

Walk Time 2hrs 10min **Distance 5.3miles/8.1km**

Start The Tavern Car Park, Thatchers Lane. GR. 323595

1. From the **CP** on Thatchers Lane, walk to the main **RD** beside Tavern pub, turn **LT** towards Matlock. Continue past the Royal Oak pub then just round the bend is a **PF** off to the **RT**. Do not take that one but the one opposite on the **LT** at the wooden **PF** sign.

2. Ascend a steep driveway, continuing to the **LT** of a short row of houses. You come to some garages as you walk up and over the brow of the hill by a stone wall. At a **PF** sign continue on to Hilltop Farm on your **LT**.

3. On reaching the farm, look for an opening on **RT** between bushes just before farm gate. Go through opening and turn **LT** behind the farm. Look ahead for openings in walls, crossing three fields. There are good views now of Matlock. After the third field turn sharply **LT**, go through a kissing gate to ascend a narrow winding path to top between a wood of young trees.

4. The path runs close to a wall along the top, with excellent views. Continue along ridge between bracken to an opening in the wall then ascend to a kissing gate and on to the top. Go through a gate on the **LT** just before Riber Castle. You walk to the **RT** of Riber Hall Farm then on a narrow path to emerge on an access **RD** beside a telephone box.

5. Turn **LT** then first **RT** around the houses, walk along the **RD** passing Riber Hall Hotel, and walk ahead to Hearthstone Lane where you turn **LT** along to Hearthstone Farm. Continue past farm still on the lane, you come to a cattle grid, turn **RT** ascending the **RT** side of a wood. Stay on this path over the brow of the hill and down to a wood on the **RT** side.

6. Opposite this wood is a waymark post and stile. Cross here into a field and continue to far corner where you start to descend steeply. A post with an arrow on it points **RT**. Go just past the farm gate and turn **RT**, walking along the field to the hedge and on to Coombs Wood.

7. At the side of the wood, turn **LT**, descend the field steeply then diagonally **LT** to Low Lees Farm below. At the outbuilding of the farm, bear **RT** on a path for a short distance then **LT** into woodland. Continue through woodland following yellow dots and arrows to an opening in a wall. Continue still on the path, over stepping-stones to ascend over a step stile up to a **RD**.

8. Go diagonally **RT** over the **RD** then over a stile there to ascend steeply to the top corner of the field by a small building and onto the **RD** at the top. Continue in same direction, passing Lea Green Development and Conference Centre. Pass the Coach House Restaurant and Jug and Glass pub.

9. A **PF** sign on **LT** states Dethick and Tansley. Go through a kissing gate there to descend a flight of steps into Swinepark Wood, over a **FB** then up more steps taking you out of the wood. Cross a step stile and follow a narrow path by a wall, crossing fields to ascend to the church at Dethick, which you should see ahead. Nearby here is the family home of Florence Nightingale.

10. Follow path through St. Johns churchyard and the village, in same direction to the **RD**. Cross **RD** following the **PF** sign there over several fields in same direction. You see a small copse ahead and your path takes you to the **LT** corner of it. You come to another **PF**, turn **RT** walking to the **RD**.

11. At **RD** turn **LT** for 80Mts then **RT** following a sign taking you back to Tansley over a series of fields. You should see the buildings ahead. You emerge by a bungalow where you cross the driveway and down the access **RD**, turning first **LT** along Starth Lane then first **RT** back to the **CP**.

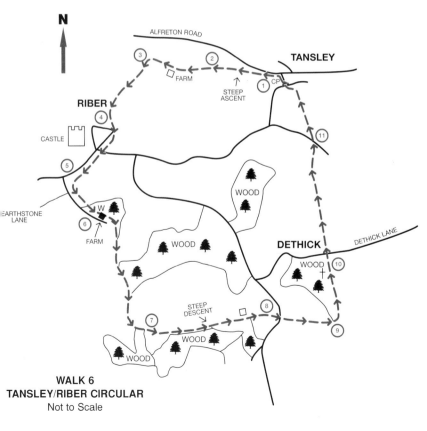

WALK 6
TANSLEY/RIBER CIRCULAR
Not to Scale

Walk 7 Winster/Luntor Rocks

Walk Time 3hrs   **Distance** 5.6miles/9km

Start Car Park beside the recycling bank on south side of Winster. GR. 239603

1. Turn LT out of the recycling bank CP across the RD from East Bank Farm and Miners Standard pub, keep LT where the RDs merge. Continue along the RD then turn LT onto the Limestone Way (opposite a lead ore house).

2. You are now walking on a track between two stone walls. You come to a stile beside a farm gate, cross and continue by the wire fence and broken stone wall. As you approach some trees nearing Luntor Rocks, bear slightly LT to go through a kissing gate. Continue through a gate at far side of copse at Luntor Rocks then 50Mts past the gate go over a stile on RT then bear LT alongside the wall.

3. Continue over four fields before branching RT across a field. Look for worn grass path and continue through openings in fields to emerge on a RD. Turn LT on RD, walking for 50Mts, an opening leads RT on a worn grass path ascending diagonally across a field. Continue in same direction through openings between fields and cross a stile to emerge on an old lane.

4. Turn LT then immediately RT onto a wider dusty lane called Blakelow Lane then LT after 15Mts following a yellow arrow on a waymark post. You are soon on a gentle descent by a broken stone wall on your RT. Stay on path crossing fields, looking ahead for openings, to an old lane called Moorlands Lane.

5. Turn LT then soon after RT. Continue a gentle descent over a series of fields keeping the wall or fence line to your RT. You see another waymarker post by a stile, cross and turn RT still descending the hill in the same direction. You are now on an overgrown lane between two stone walls. Continue down this lane through several farm gates then as you approach the buildings at the bottom, turn RT through an opening in the stone wall following a PF sign.

6. The path veers diagonally LT across the field. Look for the narrow opening in the lower half of the field. Cross and stay on the worn path to descend to a lane, keeping Bromlea Farm off to your LT. On the lane turn RT then LT after 50Mts to take you over a series of eight fields. You emerge on another PF.

7. Descending the hill you pass some trees then look for a waymarker with three arrows on it. A stile is to the LT of it and you go across it to ascend the next hillside. Look for another waymarker as you ascend into woodland. Nearing the brow of the hill, you come to a wide grass track. Go straight across over a broken wall then bear LT to take you to the LT of Bottom Leys Farm, which you should see ahead.

8. Cross the stile in front of the farm, continue in same direction up to a farm access **RD** then to the minor **RD**. Continue across onto Green Lane (track). Walking along the lane you see a quarry ahead. Before descending the far side of the lane, turn **RT** on a **PF** to take you to the **RT** of Whitelow Farm, continuing over a stile ahead up to a lane.

9. On the lane, bear **RT** for 185Mts then **LT** on a **PF** towards Winster. You continue now for $3/4$ mile on a long straight walk across fields. As you draw parallel with Moor Farm on your **RT**, bear **RT** through an opening then **LT** following the path towards a minor **RD**.

10. At Bonsall Lane, turn **LT** for 140Mts then **RT** through a narrow opening into a field. Ascend field before veering **LT** near the top. Continue descending far side, crossing fields to join the path you originally started on. Turn **LT** back to main **RD** then **RT** back to the **CP**.

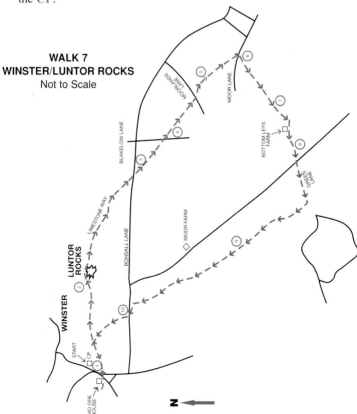

WALK 7
WINSTER/LUNTOR ROCKS
Not to Scale

Walk 8 Ashford in the Water
Walk Time 2hrs 15min   **Distance** 5.8miles/9.3km
Start Beside the Ashford Arms in Ashford in the Water.
GR. 197697

1. Walk along Greaves Lane opposite, the **RD** bends **RT** then **LT** at the top ascending gradually. The path disappears but stay on the **RT** side of the **RD** going over the brow of the hill. You see some houses and barns on the **RT** and a **PF** sign to Monsal Head along a narrow path to the **RT**. Follow this path, in a straight line through openings and small gates into several fields to emerge on a lane.

2. Cross the lane through a narrow opening following the sign to Monsal Head. On a worn narrow path over a field, go through small gates and over stone steps into fields, still in a straight line.

3. You come to a disused railway line, turn **LT** then **RT** crossing stone steps, following a **PF** sign for Little Longstone and Monsal Head. Follow the worn path descending the field then cross the next field bearing **RT** on the obvious path up towards Little Longstone, which you can see ahead.

4. As you approach the gate and **RD** in Little Longstone, do not go through onto the **RD** but turn immediately **RT** following the sign and feint path bearing **RT** towards Gt. Longstone. Ascend the hillside to top of field crossing a stile then through an opening into next field.

5. You are now on level ground as you diagonally cross a field then cross a farm access track and through two small gates over next fields. You should see the village of Gt. Longstone ahead as you cross fields. On reaching the **RD** beside the houses, turn **RT** and walk down the **RD**. As you reach the last street on the **LT**, called Glebe Ave, turn along it, in front of the houses.

6. Walk to the far end and as you pass Furnell Ave, look for a **PF** sign on **RT**. Follow this through the farm gate then turn diagonally **LT** across the field to a small gate in the hedge. Cross the next field and through another gate. Follow the **PF** sign there in same direction to lower far corner of field. Just before you get there you cross another **PF** from **LT** to **RT**. Turn **RT** there walking a short distance to the opening onto the railway embankment.

7. On reaching the embankment path, turn **LT** and walk for 920Mts, crossing bridges over two **RDs**. You see a house on **LT** across a field and as you draw level with it, a **PB** sign points **RT** to Bakewell. Turn **RT** here through a gate then along between two stone walls, gradually ascending, going through a 5-bar gate and over the brow of the hill. Keep on this path to Bakewell, ignoring all other paths.

8. You descend to Bakewell on a wide grass field then stony access track emerging near some houses. Turn **RT** on the lane at the bottom then cross a stone **FB** over the river, to emerge on the main A6 **RD**. Turn **RT** on main **RD** walking on footpath at side of A6 **RD**. Pass Riverside Business Park on your **RT** then Deepdale Business Park on the **LT**.

9. Just opposite is a small opening on your **RT** leading into a field. Follow the worn narrow path to walk between the houses and cross a **RD**. Continue over several fields on undulating path in same direction nearby the river towards Ashford. Pass a waterfall on **RT** and through a gate leading to the river then to the main A6 **RD**.

10. Turn **RT** at the **RD** and **RT** again soon after to cross the bridge over the river. Cross the **RD** with care at the far side and continue back to the Ashford Arms pub in Ashford.

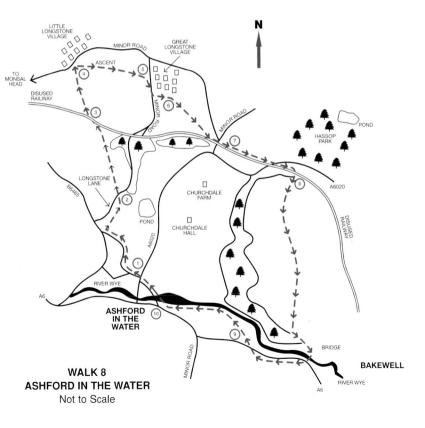

WALK 8
ASHFORD IN THE WATER
Not to Scale

Walk 9 Jughole Wood & Wensley Round
Walk Time 4hrs   **Distance** 6.4miles/10.3km
Start On Matlock Bridge in Centre. GR. 298602

1. Starting on the bridge in Matlock centre, take RT fork passing The Royal Bank of Scotland on your RT. In a short distance you see a sign for the Limestone Way, ascending steeply LT on a track. Ascend here passing a row of houses then alongside a farm. Continue ascending in a straight line up through a narrow opening between a stone wall into a field.

2. Now ascend on a grass path. Looking back you have an excellent view of Matlock as you pass a post with yellow arrows on it. Stay in same direction and where path forks, carry straight on. You see County Offices off to LT. Go through another narrow opening onto a lane, carrying straight across through an opening between the hedge.

3. Soon you cross a stile still ascending, continue following a white arrow along the side of a field. Go through the narrow openings in the stone walls as you cross several fields, still ascending gradually. You see Mason Lees Farm ahead on LT as you climb the fields, go through the gate leading up towards the farm.

4. Keep straight ahead with the hedge line just on your RT. Look ahead for an opening at the top side of the field between two posts leading onto the farm access RD. Cross the access RD, the ascent is steep up the next field. Pass a farm on LT as you ascend the small field where a gate is in the RT corner with an arrow on it.

5. Continue through to ascend steeply to trees at the top. Keep the hedge line on your RT side then cross stile at top RT corner of field. You now emerge on a lane following the Limestone Way RT for 16Mts then turn LT by a wooden seat and go through a metal gate. You ascend a slightly worn grass path over the side of the hill.

6. On the far side of the hill you pass some large stones, go over a stile on RT into the next field following a path off to LT to an opening in a stone wall. This brings you onto another farm access track which you cross into next field. You are now on level ground walking across the centre of a field.

7. You pass an underground reservoir on your LT then come to an opening in a stone wall. Continue in a straight line towards a small barn ahead then as you pass the barn your path bears off RT to cross an opening onto an old lane. As you emerge on this old lane, look straight across for an opening and stile with yellow arrows on far side. Cross the stile then bear RT across a field on bearing 2°M, this takes you through into next field.

8. Keep a stone wall on your **RT** as you come to a minor **RD**, cross it then cross a stile to descend a field. You see a small radio mast on your **RT**. Cross a stile into Jughole Wood. Your path bears **LT** as you descend steeply. Cross a stile leading out of the wood.

9. Look for a feint worn path as you continue diagonally **RT** across a field. You see Leewood Farm at bottom of hillside and a cottage ahead to your **LT**. Head for the cottage before branching off **LT**. Follow the narrow cow track and continue descending gently on the path, then as you approach level with the cottage, your path bears off **LT** towards a small wood you can see ahead.

10. Walk to the **LT** of the wood as you ascend to the top of the hill. Look for an opening at top with two yellow arrows on it. Continue in same direction up to level ground. From the post there, bear 206°M. Continue over two large fields through two metal gates and past a barn onto a **RD**. Reaching the **RD**, turn immediately **RT** then **RT** again onto an overgrown path.

11. Approx 23**Mts** along the path, look for a narrow opening on **RT** in the hedge leading into a field. Cross this and several further fields through narrow openings, as you descend the path disappears. The village of Wensley is below in the valley with a hill to the **RT** of it.

12. Descend steeply to the lower **LT** corner of field, cross a stile following a path through the bracken. Cross another stile bearing **RT** descending towards Wensley. As you reach level ground further on, the path divides in a field that has a broken stone wall around it. Bear **RT** at the far side; look for a small opening in the wall. Do not follow **LT** fork leading past a barn.

13. The path is not visible but head for the row of houses you should see ahead. You descend steeply again before a short section takes you to the bottom of a narrow valley. Cross to a gate by a rock face and walk through towards the houses. You emerge on a **RD** by a row of houses then cross onto a short tarmac path taking you to the **RT** of the church.

14. You come to South Darley C of E school and the church, turn **RT** on the **RD** in front of the school. Walk down the short lane then turn **LT** taking you to the main **RD**. Continue down the main **RD** and walk past the Three Stags Heads pub, crossing a bridge over the River Derwent to the Square and Compasses pub at the far side.

15. There are two **PFs** next to each other to the **RT** of the pub. Take the **RT** path, which has a wooden arrow stating **PF** up to a farm. Walk in front of the farm continuing over several fields in a straight line. Approaching trees at the far end look for an opening in the **LT** corner of the stone wall. Cross into next field then follow worn grass path across to the River Derwent.

16. Approaching the far side of the field you see the river on the **RT** then you go through an opening and bear **RT** along the side of the field. Cross a stile then cross over a small **FB** before continuing on a path along by the river then by the railway line. Walk through a series of fields between the river and the railway line, keeping near the railway line.

17. You pass by two railway underpasses but continue keeping railway on **LT**. As you approach the end of the fields, there are some concrete ladder steps on **LT**. Cross then turn **RT** on the path at side of the railway.

18. You come to a level crossing with a farm gate at each side, go over to far side, watch for trains. You emerge on the A6 by houses, turn **RT**, walking along the **RD** back into Matlock.

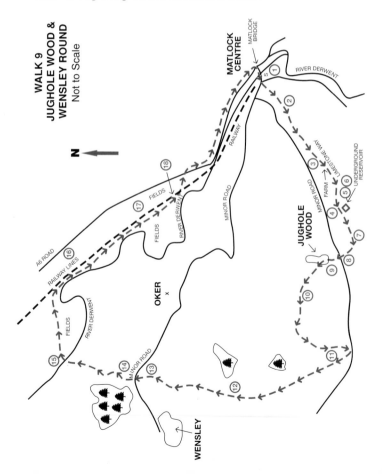

WALK 9
JUGHOLE WOOD &
WENSLEY ROUND
Not to Scale